How to
Baptize
a Child
in Flint,
Michigan

ALSO BY SARAH CARSON

Buick City

How to Baptize a Child in Flint, Michigan

Poems

Sarah Carson

A Karen & Michael Braziller Book
PERSEA BOOKS / NEW YORK

Persea Books, Inc.
90 Broad Street
New York, New York 10004

Library of Congress Cataloging-in-Publication Data
Names: Carson, Sarah, 1984– author.
Title: How to baptize a child in Flint, Michigan : poems / Sarah Carson.
Other titles: How to baptize a child in Flint, Michigan (Compilation)
Description: New York : Persea Books, [2022] | "A Karen & Michael Braziller
    Book." | Summary: "Spanning girlhood to motherhood, How to Baptize a Child
    in Flint, Michigan traces the lineage of four generations of a Flint, Michigan
    family—from the trailer park to the factory floor to, perhaps, a future far away.
    These poems examine the wreckage of the American Dream and ask who will
    answer for the promises we were made to believe as children: God? Industry?
    America? If we are all a part of the problem, are we are also all a part of the
    cure?"—Provided by publisher.
Identifiers: LCCN 2022019038 | ISBN 9780892555635 (paperback)
Subjects: LCSH: Flint (Mich.)—Poetry. | LCGFT: Poetry.
Classification: LCC PS3603.A77627 H69 2022 | DDC 811/.6—dc23/eng/20220502
LC record available at https://lccn.loc.gov/2022019038

Book design and composition by Rita Lascaro
Manufactured in the United States of America.

for Z

CONTENTS

AUTHOR'S NOTE

Father Thomas Keating wrote, "If you accept the belief that baptism incorporates us in the mystical body of Christ, into the divine DNA, then you might say that the Holy Spirit is present in each of us, and thus we have the capacity for the fullness of redemption, of transformation."

The poems in this book are my own prayers for the fullness of redemption in my life and in the lives of the people I love. They are based on true events, but they are in no way meant to be a definitive or comprehensive account of what it means to be from any one place.

Flint, Michigan is a place of beauty and fullness, as well as grief that spans generations. If we are to hope for transformation in Flint and in places like it, I believe it begins with seeing the Spirit in each of us, acknowledging the systemic injustices that include racism, greed and indifference, and living into the baptismal promise to "care for others and the world God made, and work for justice and peace" (*Evangelical Lutheran Worship*, p. 228).

Where They Don't Name Streets for Us

This neighborhood, these boulevards,
these streets named for carburetors

where some kids whiled out
school days, centuries,

these avenues barely know the sound
of one box truck from another,

you, me from other girls,
early spring shoots of grass

for whom neighbor boys' long legs
count cement stoops,

whose daddies warm
motorcycles on the driveway,

whose mommas can't leave
their card tables,

tell these men to ride along.
When we were young,

we dug tombs
beneath burning barrels,

left waving flags
for other kids.

Now the patrolmen in the park
would not know our names

if a dispatcher spelled them
letter by letter.

Now these girls, these boys
have not found one remnant of us:

not one foul word
we wrote

in wet cement,
not one foul ball

we did not chase
into the street.

In the city where we were born,
God set a star

above the river,
as if to leave a light on,

as if we could
come home again.

But now we are
the strangers.

The garage where we
burned evenings

has left town
2 x 4 by 2 x 4.

Even stray dogs won't take
scraps from our hands.

Ode to Flint, Michigan, Five Years, Three Months, Ten Days after the Water Crisis Began

In the city where I was born,
my daughter cannot

use the water:
to rinse her curls

could stop her growing,
slam the storm doors shut.

Where I've dreamed
her tall,

eclipsed by daylight,
this city follows,

every shadow
unmoving.

I take my things
to the map edge,

& the city comes home
shouting.

Police on the lawn.
City with coals for hands.

City, city
everywhere

& not a drop
to drink.

Don't Touch

The first gun we knew came in a toolbox for the
apocalypse: hammer, barrel, crushed can, pack of
Newports, a ballpoint pen someone took apart. Momma
said, *Don't touch* & we didn't—because all that could
happen next seemed obvious: blue lights in the
windows of houses already turned out for the evening,
boys with pockets clenched in their fists. Brother
says it was there—next to the TV remotes, the box of
tissues—that the pistol became a whole thing. One boy
grabbed at another's t-shirt & the sounds that came
next were fire spreading up a staircase, the sounds of a
freight train with a cement block in its tracks. The gun
was afraid of nothing—not daylight, not trouble—
& Brother palmed it like he was drawing from a stack
of discards. When one boy jumped another, opened his
temple onto concrete, where earlier in the afternoon
two boys shot rock, shot scissors, soon there were
spiderweb cracks in the laundromat window, holes just
big enough to fit our fingers. There were stray shells
that needed picking from the grass before another girl
showed up with a lawnmower. *Don't touch*, we told kids
riding big wheels in nothing but diapers & sunglasses,
kids with whole collections of shells in shoeboxes. *Don't
touch*, we told the dog, his muzzle a divining rod, his
body a strung bow.

On the Playground, Brother Teaches the Old Testament

On the third day, Brother says,
God created opportunity.

He retells Joshua,
& the walls stay up.

There's a hole in Rahab's floor
for cigarettes & rum.

God does not send Jonah
to Nineveh.

God sends Daddy to get Uncle
from the White Horse.

There are new
commandments:

Don't leave your shadow
for the darkness,

cross the older boys
only once.

Brother dips a finger
in the fountain.

Lunch Lady calls him,
Problem.

Says *Boys like you
become*

*chalk marks
on a wall.*

Girls in the bleachers
hold their breath

like sacrifice
can save him.

Brother has not gotten to Job,
Isaiah.

Brother has not covered
salvation yet.

If the Pontiac Broke Down

No combination of car door,
tire iron,

rolled up window
was safety.

South of the mailboxes,
the boxelder tree,

the box truck
now half-empty,

there was no justice
but a broken bottle,

a length of razor wire
beneath the Slip 'N Slide.

Maybe this is why Momma
took us to church,

barretted our hair
on the porch Daddy built

using the hand
he did not slice open

with the post hole
digger,

had us sing Nahum, Habakkuk,
Micah, Amos

until we found chapter & verse
faster than God.

When summer came,
when uncles gathered at the river,

Momma held us
to her thigh as warning,

Touch them
& you will not touch another:

another PBR,
another paper plate,

as if to say,
You are not my brothers

but a fire I intend
to put out.

Maybe this is why Pentecost
is the cruelest season:

revival songs, one-pieces,
an eight-fingered man

who sells fireworks
from a tow-trailer.

Maybe this is why
Momma doesn't drink from the cup.

Maybe this is why
This is my body

is the only prayer
Momma ever believed.

Ode to Brother's Best Friend in the Trailer Park

What is a trailer park
anyway

if not tire fire,
burning barrel,

somebody's stolen
license plate?

Somebody's empty
vape pen stuck

in somebody's
grandma's door?

Brother's coming back
from the liquor store.

The kids are shut
on the porch again.

A truck pulls up
to the curb

like a lightning storm,
& even the plastic

on the window
can't breathe.

Girls dream
he trips

a speed trap,
dots a deputy flashlight.

He is a dog whistle.
A line other boys don't cross.

The D.A. is barely listening
if she says,

Tell me everything
you remember.

I remember:
knuckle, valley,

soft indents
along a hipbone,

a mirror where
the bed fit.

His reflection
an empty bowl—

the exclamation points
of his temples

as if to say,
End the story here.

When I Am 14½ Years Old,
Brother Gets Taken in for Questioning

How many rounds, a deputy asks,

can a Patriot hold?

The answer is what every schoolboy

from here to Sanilac

has always known:

that a boy on a bridge in the dark

must return to the truck

like a homing pigeon,

or else keep his rations close—

a sweatshirt still soft

from the tumble dry

where on other nights

other girls

burrowed against wind,

shadow of moon

on roller coaster,

the midway

a mark between

the here & thereafter—

where elsewhere a flashlight

floods the bluestem,

crickets scatter.

Brother watches

a line of cars

crest one stanchion,

then another

while all the other

girls we've known

let their wild hair

free

in the sky

behind them

& scream.

Ode to the City That Is Not My City

Dear city
I am not from,

without you,
I'm from Eden.

My other city
sent a serpent,

dressed a ghost
in warmer clothes.

Two boys
walk bikes

through a
parking lot,

this city
demands

their boombox.
She is moving grass,

a promise
breaking.

She's made up
her mind:

No one leaves
for free.

Six Reasons I Can't Answer the Door for Him at 3 in the Morning

The last man here wanted
what could not be taken:

My girl, he'd say,
my baby.

The narrow of his eyes
scattered mice in the walls.

The man before him
hid cans in high cabinets.

Neighbors slipped notes through
the breezeway:

Just yell help,
they said.

Police are quick
here—

here as in
not someplace else.

Then there's Brother,
who can't come home at Christmas.

The girl he swears he doesn't know
in my same sweatshirt

when they pull her
from the creek.

In the city
where we were born,

bullets crawl blocks
like brush fire,

spent casings
end up in water.

Police come
to the door,

ask for men
who've said our names.

Now—tucked between
my hip bone & my ribcage—

I'm growing
another body.

The dark cloud
of the ultrasound

says she'll be
a girl like me.

If we believe
what God says

about Adam's
rib bone,

about his
finger-pointing,

we know
it falls to girls

to pass the
warning:

There are men
who sleep &

men who can't and
it's up to us

to know
the difference.

It's up to us
to know

a door is also
a thing that opens,

even a deadbolt is still
a kind of hope.

Baby, Your Daddy Called to
Say He Gave Us Chlamydia

I told him, *No, sweetheart.*
You gave us the world.

Now angels are downstairs
breaking bottles on the banister.

Wise men trip an alarm
drunk on Godiva & rum.

All our lives
we've been told

a December baby
could save us.

Now unto us, this night,
in the city of accidents,

shepherds tend
pocket holes—

leave the body
to weed

& it grows
what it wants.

Even if others could not,
you, little soul,

will make a go of it,
Queen Esther

with a hand-drawn map
to the king's chambers.

The story of exile
is written in your muscles,

says a city's walls
are not stronger than its trumpets,

says a star will
lead us home again.

The promised land
is real.

How to Baptize a Child in Flint, Michigan

First, hold the curve
of their head like

packed snow,
a struck match,

a field mouse
you catch

with the cup
of your hand.

Say they can be anything,
refill their root beer;

tell them,
Yes,

people like us
can be great, too.

If you're going
to the firehouse,

bring them with you;
say, *God is good,*

even if a guardsman
says otherwise.

At home,
dinner in the microwave,

Mountain Dew
& TV light,

when the textbook insists
we are already water

say, *Of course
we are, boo,*

though you don't know
the specifics,

just that Pastor says river
is a holy thing;

Jesus himself
could walk it in bare feet.

On Easter, when they
fall asleep

during altar call,
when they wake

& whisper,
What is brimstone?

What's repentance?
Send them out to the narthex,

ask them if they're thirsty.
Tell them,

These reckoning songs
are not for us.

It's 3:45 in the Morning & I'm Thinking of All the Mothers who Are Not Awake Now

Mothers who can't wake, or won't
(if there's a difference)—

mother of GIRL WITH AUTISM
TAKEN FROM HOME

AFTER FATHER CATCHES MOTHER
FEEDING GIRL BLEACH.

Daughter of mother
of so many other

sopping wet sobbing nights
is about to wake

& I'm awake, anticipating,
& I don't know

why we are us instead of
MOTHER KNOWINGLY AND INTENTIONALLY

DEPRIVED SON OF NECESSITIES,
if it's something I've done,

or she has,
a lucky guess,

a right turn where
the road ran out beneath the sky.

My mother says, *It's those*
who cared for us once,

spooned our own milk
into bottles,

but mother of MOTHER ARRAIGNED
IN DEATH OF FIVE-MONTH-OLD

surely had her own
long nights,

her own milk
dripping on the carpet.

So what, then,
of other girls

in other bassinets,
other mothers

still sound asleep
or sound awake elsewhere?

Where is mother of
BEATEN 3-YEAR-OLD

ON LIFE SUPPORT—
& who will go looking

except for the moon?
The sheriff?

Is she so far we have not
bumped car doors,

switched seats at a hockey game?
Promise me, love,

she is so, so different
than we.

Ode to the City That Is Not My City

Dear city
I am not from,

without you,
I'm from nowhere.

My other city called me
home again,

threw the truck keys
in the creek.

I give her
what she asks for,

but every
evening is a set fire.

Her eyes
are open wounds.

Her mouth
is danger.

She'd leave the baby
in the pool

to finish a fight
in the street.

It's May in Flint, Michigan & We Skip Work to Watch Air Force One Descend Over the City

In the city where we were born
girls take inventory of disaster:

one solder burn,
one pen knife,

one tattoo
of a ghost.

After a year full of winter,
dogs' teeth find leaves,

vines,
stray roots

where there once was
a kind of optimism.

Old men on
slumped stoops

say, *At least we're here
to tell the story* &

they do not mean,
Praise be.

They mean: *What I would not
give for.*

They mean: *Every other small thing
has also grown & grown.*

A List of Things I Hope You'll Understand about Everyone I Knew in the 21st Century

When we were born, we were starlight: made to sparkle, bent on waning.

.

They said we had 80 years, 40 if the ice caps really did melt.

.

There's no picture of the night Dan Miller kissed me on the back porch of his mother's rented duplex. It was summer, and the box elder bugs marched the curve of our unfinished bodies. You may find this unremarkable, but without this, I doubt you'd exist.

.

We did know we were made of stuff other suns shoot from their spindly edges: light, hunger, infinity, cell phone signals.

.

But YouTube was still new. The glowing could still keep us awake.

•

I'm sure your museums have exhibits dedicated to
that which sustained us: the AM/FM radio, microwave
popcorn, a Chevy Cavalier someone rolled out of the
woods like a boulder.

•

What you could not know about these things, however,
is what we never knew until we lost them, the way a
slow song hummed through a dashboard, the smell of
smoke coming from somewhere far away.

•

So you've heard we let children carry boxcutters into
cafeterias & you might think we could have done more
to stop it. But it'd be a mistake to think we would
have given up all off this to go back to 1995, to sit at
the cement lip of the garage as the rain came in from
across the river, the living room curtains billowing, the
phone ringing from somewhere deep inside the house,
something inside you sure that someone was definitely,
absolutely calling for you.

Picking up a Prescription for My Daughter
at the Rite Aid That Replaced the Rite Aid where
My Mother Picked up Prescriptions for Me

Maybe there is no explaining
how a patch of grass was once

not a patch of grass—
if it took twenty years

to tear down, erect
one building,

it also took twenty years
to sell the house on Seymour,

pack the soup spoons,
the sandwich maker—

move, move again,
move back.

In the place where a doctor
once splinted

my ring & pinkie fingers
together,

where my mother once
rocked my sister in a stationary chair,

imagine a soft tuft of bunny
burrows in tall grass,

a single bee makes a break
for dandelion heads.

Where once a pharmacist
shifted weight

between pill bottles,
bandages,

a doe leads her fawn
through fir needles,

a birch branch
breaks, remains.

Where once a display
of cough syrup

took the shape
of a Christmas tree,

a celebration,
I am emerging

through touchless
sliding doors,

plastic bags full of
half-off Halloween candy,

a humidifier
for the long night to follow.

I am telling
my daughter

my mother was also
a girl once

nestled in
a lap

that would one day
nestle me,

would one day
nestle her.

Brother Says in 1996, He Saw His Buddy Shoot A Girl

I say, Oh, love,
I say, oh no,

oh God, no,
you didn't.

I say, maybe if you think
about it,

you only dreamed
you did.

I say, maybe if you
think about it

you'll decide
you thought

he could have
& imagined it.

I say, maybe,
worst case scenario,

there were a lot of accidents
that year.

I say, no, love,
you didn't see

your buddy
shoot a girl,

you saw Independence Day
& got a little too excited.

You saw the brick
blow out of the federal building.

You saw America,
& thought,

Well, this must be
all there is.

GG turned out
the hallway light

& a flash
of filament

stung your eyes
before you

creeped out
the garage window.

You saw your buddy
across the watermelon field

& thought,
Who are you

to pull so much
good fruit from the vine?

No, love,
you did not see

your buddy
shoot a girl

because I saw you
shoot her:

once to cut
her down.

Six more for the place
in the small of her back

she never let anyone
touch.

I saw you do it
like I saw you

cradle the dog
where the grass

met the
creekbed.

I saw you do it in
every

photograph,
in every letter

you've sent
home.

Ode to Flint, Michigan on December 30, 2014,
the 78th Anniversary of the Great Sit-down Strike

This city is a fire
extinguished, reignited.

Scraped knee,
skinned knuckle—

she loves
a good fight.

This morning
she's on the back stoop

listening to archival tape
of our grandfathers:

me & three or four other guys
climbed the gate, they say.

They'd been making weapons
out of spare parts:

A great slingshot
to throw heavy things.

The story we know best,
of course,

is the one in which
our fate reverses.

There were whole years
where we rode our bikes uphill

if only to turn around
and look back.

Now I dream of other towns &
this city shakes me upright,

says, *You were saying
their names again.*

Fine, city.
Sit, I say,

*hang your jacket
on the porchrail.*

*Put another 2x4
on the fire.*

It is not
without precedent,

after all, that we just might
save ourselves.

Brother Gets Transferred Out of
Solitary & Swears Jesus Planned It All

The letter arrives
already opened,

already redacted,
says we could get a call

at Christmas
this year.

I don't ask,
What was Christmas

to Mary's son
anyway?

Where is Bethlehem
to a city kid?

Where were wise men
when we also needed

gold, would have settled
for myrrh?

I don't ask why
no one in B Unit

knows Jesus was born
in August

because it'd be a mistake
to blame this on Jesus, anyway—

even if Brother swears
by the Sermon on the Mount now,

says the whole world
is a moving star,

a specifically appointed
clearing,

how could I not say,
I know, Brother, mine, too?

Telling My Daughter the Story of the Woman at the Well

We cannot count the ways
we may have never existed,

the improbability
of our grandmothers—

women who picked & packed
pieces of the future.

Here a warm quilt.
There a child who could read.

GG says
if she'd had a choice in it,

there'd have been
far fewer babies,

bottles boiling
in the stock pot.

Your grandfather,
sixth of seven,

carries this knowledge
in his knuckles.

In what photos remain
there is no sidewalk yet.

His sneakers scratch
the cement stoop

like a loose boat scrapes
a dam.

So his mother
can't explain

how quickly the future
becomes what happened,

how the what-nows &
the how-comes

turn into stories
we refuse to speak.

Think of it:
For how many centuries

did a girl go
to the well,

go to the well again,
go to the well again

before a stranger
stopped her,

insisted on telling
her fortune?

So later
he exits a tomb

as if by some kind
miracle.

Who's to say
that we won't also?

Every day
women split

themselves
open

so that the future
can begin again.

ACKNOWLEDGMENTS

Thank you to the following publications in which these poems—in one form or another—previously appeared: *the Baltimore Review, The Christian Century, Cincinnati Review, Colorado Review, Copper Nickel, East Village Magazine, Epiphany, the Journal, Laurel Review, Lumina, Rattle, Solstice, Sonora Review, Superstition Review, Typo* and *Waxwing*.

This book also owes a special debt of gratitude to Liv Larson Andrews, whose poem, "How to Baptize a Child in Flint, Michigan," inspired the poem of the same title for which this collection is named.

Finally, this book would not exist without the love and patience of my po-group—Margaret Brady, Bill Coughlin, Carol Eding and Joe Eldridge; the other half of the Thursday night, Flint-area writing collective, Nic Custer; the long weekend Nancy Tancredi hosted by the ocean where Penny Guisinger laughed at my jokes and Tessa Mellas played the piano; kind and careful readings by Jan Worth-Nelson and Dennis Hinrichsen; Pastor Betty Landis and Ralph Hamilton who both told me to stop obsessing and have courage; and, of course, my mom, her mother's mom, my father's mom and all the moms before them and beside them who were just doing their very best to get through each day.

SOME RESOURCES TOWARD TRANSFORMATION IN FLINT, MICHIGAN

If you'd like to learn more about the ongoing pursuit of transformation in Flint, the following resources are a good start:

BOOKS

Stereo(TYPE) by Jonah Mixon-Webster

What the Eyes Don't See: A Story of Crisis, Resistance, and Hope in an American City by Mona Hanna-Attisha

The Poisoned City by Anna Clark

Demolition Means Progress: Flint, Michigan, and the Fate of the American Metropolis by Andrew Highsmith

Flint Fights Back: Environmental Justice and Democracy in the Flint Water Crisis by Benjamin J. Pauli

ORGANIZATIONS

The Flint Registry, www.flintregistry.org

The Flint Kids Fund, www.flintkids.org

The Flint River Watershed Coalition, www.flintwaterstudy.org

ABOUT THE LEXI RUDNITSKY EDITOR'S CHOICE AWARD

The Lexi Rudnitsky Editor's Choice Award is given annually to a poetry collection by a writer who has published at least once previous book of poems. Along with the Lexi Rudnitsky First Book Prize in Poetry, it is a collaboration of Persea Books and the Lexi Rudnitsky Poetry Project. Entry guidelines for both awards are available on Persea's website (www.perseabooks.com).

Lexi Rudnitsky (1972–2005) grew up outside of Boston, and studied at Brown University and Columbia University. Her own poems exhibit both a playful love of language and a fierce conscience. Her writing appeared in *The Antioch Review, Columbia: A Journal of Literature and Art, The Nation, The New Yorker, The Paris Review, Pequod,* and *The Western Humanities Review.* In 2004, she won the Milton Kessler Memorial Prize for Poetry from *Harpur Palate.*

Lexi died suddenly in 2005, just months after the birth of her first child and the acceptance for publication of her first book of poems, *A Doorless Knocking into Night* (MidList Press, 2006). The Lexi Rudnitsky book prizes were created to memorialize her by promoting the type of poet and poetry in which she so spiritedly believed.

Previous winners of the Lexi Rudnitsky Editor's Choice Award:

2020	Christopher Salerno, *The Man Grave*
2019	Enid Shomer, *Shoreless*
2018	Cameron Awkward-Rich, *Dispatch*
2017	Gary Young, *That's What I Thought*
2016	Heather Derr-Smith, *Thrust*
2015	Shane McCrae *The Animal Too Big to Kill*
2014	Caki Wilkinson, *The Wynona Stone Poems*
2013	Michael White, *Vermeer in Hell*
2012	Mitchell L. H. Douglas, *blak al-febet*
2011	Amy Newman, *Dear Editor*